SCIENCE QUEST

AMAZON ADVENTURE

QEB

QEB Publishing

DAN
GREEN

Cover Design: Mandy Norman
Illustrator: Damien Jones
Editor: Amanda Askew
Designer: Punch Bowl Design
QEB Project Editor: Ruth Symons
Managing Editor: Victoria Garrard
Design Manager: Anna Lubecka

First published in the US in 2013 by
QEB Publishing, Inc.
3 Wrigley, Suite A
Irvine, CA 92618

www.qed-publishing.co.uk

A CIP record for this book is available
from the Library of Congress.

ISBN 978 1 60992 506 2

Printed in China

Photo credits
Shutterstock: Anatoli Styf, 16;
Dr. Morley Read, 21; Eky Studio,
33; L.Watcharapol, 47; lelik759,
18; mexrix, 23; Rechitan Sorin, 20;
Stefano Cavoretto, 23;
Tischenko Irina, 23, 46

HOW TO BEGIN YOUR ADVENTURE

Are you ready for an amazing adventure that will test your brainpower to the limit—full of mind-bending puzzles, twists, and turns? Then this is the book for you!

Amazon Adventure is no ordinary book—you don't read the pages in order, 1, 2, 3. . . . Instead you jump forward and backward through the book as the plot unfolds. Sometimes you may lose your way, but the story will soon guide you back to where you need to be.

The story starts on page 4. Straight away, there are puzzles to solve, choices to make, and clues to pick up. The choices will look something like this:

IF YOU THINK THE CORRECT ANSWER IS A, GO TO PAGE 10

 IF YOU THINK THE CORRECT ANSWER IS B, GO TO PAGE 18

Your task is to solve each problem. So, if you think the correct answer is A, turn to page 10 and look for the same symbol in blue. That's where you will find the next part of the story.

If you make the wrong choice, the text will explain where you went wrong and let you have another chance.

The problems in this adventure are about living things, habitats, and the environment. To solve them you must use your science skills. To help you, there's a glossary of useful words at the back of the book, starting on page 44.

Are you ready? Turn the page and let your adventure begin!

AMAZON ADVENTURE

With a roar of the propeller engine, you touch down in Brazil.

Six months ago your Great Uncle Ramsey set out to look for the Lost Land of Gold, but he vanished without a trace. You've come to the rain forest along the banks of the mighty Amazon River to get to the bottom of the mystery.

With a copy of Ramsey's journal and a map in your bag, you're ready to go.

START YOUR ADVENTURE
ON PAGE 26

A bee can't make its food from sunlight, so it doesn't belong at the bottom of the pyramid.

TRY AGAIN ON PAGE 15

Correct! That's 200 billion gallons of water every hour!

You lie back and trail a hand in the water, watching the river dolphins play. Suddenly, Astro screams—a caiman is swimming behind you. Should you be worried?

YES, IT'S A **CARNIVORE.** TURN TO PAGE 19

NOT AT ALL—IT'S A **HERBIVORE.** GO TO PAGE 31

JUST BE CAUTIOUS; IT'S **AN OMNIVORE.** JUMP TO PAGE 43

No, this is a fully grown adult, ready to lay its own eggs.

GO BACK TO PAGE 11 AND **TRY AGAIN**

That's right! Humans use these antibacterial chemicals to prevent infection and to help healing.

Ramsey leads you to a small stream.

During the expedition, we couldn't see the treasure right under our noses. An undiscovered species of golden frog. The Land of Gold is right here!

Congratulations! You've found Great Uncle Ramsey.
You decide to stay a while and document all of
the amazing things he has found. When you bring
news of this undiscovered species to the world, you
will become the greatest explorer of all time!

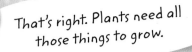
That's right. Plants need all those things to grow.

Wow! You know a lot about this place. Could you give me a few tips?

Of course. The rain forest can be dangerous if you don't understand how it works.

So, imagine there are tangled vines blocking your path. What should you do?

 GRAB HOLD AND **MOVE THEM** OUT OF THE WAY. TURN TO PAGE 20

 CARRY A STICK AND USE IT TO **PUSH THE VINES ASIDE.** TURN TO PAGE 28

 DUCK UNDERNEATH THE VINES (WITHOUT LOOKING). TURN TO PAGE 42

That's right. Plastic is man-made, not natural, so it isn't found in the Amazon.

As you walk into camp, the guides seem surprised to see you. But they're happy you've got fish and Cat starts cooking. You hang your hammock, but your mosquito net is full of holes. It was fine earlier . . .

That could be dangerous. After all, you know how many species of insect there are here, don't you?

Is it . . .

 100 OR SO? TURN TO PAGE 27

 10,000, GIVE OR TAKE A FEW? GO TO PAGE 39

 **25–30 MILLION?** TURN TO PAGE 10

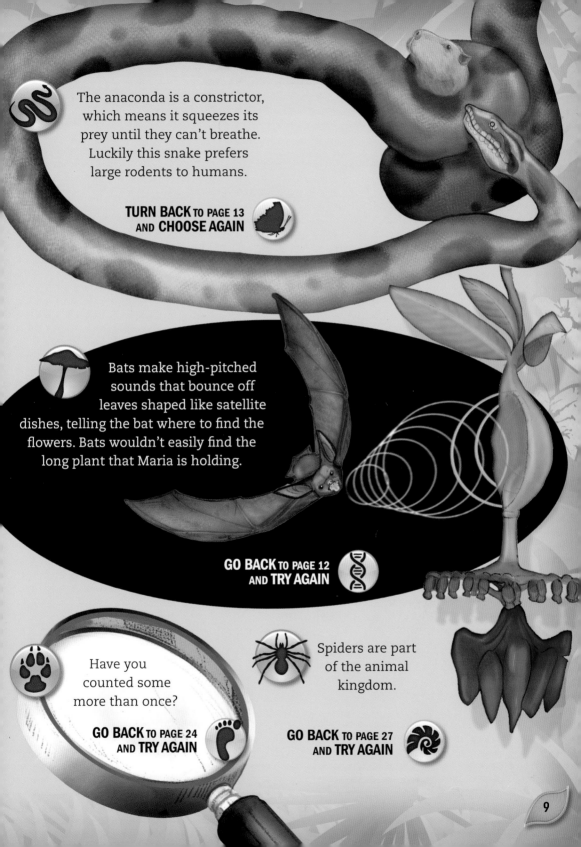

The anaconda is a constrictor, which means it squeezes its prey until they can't breathe. Luckily this snake prefers large rodents to humans.

TURN BACK TO PAGE 13 AND **CHOOSE AGAIN**

Bats make high-pitched sounds that bounce off leaves shaped like satellite dishes, telling the bat where to find the flowers. Bats wouldn't easily find the long plant that Maria is holding.

GO BACK TO PAGE 12 AND **TRY AGAIN**

Have you counted some more than once?

GO BACK TO PAGE 24 AND **TRY AGAIN**

Spiders are part of the animal kingdom.

GO BACK TO PAGE 27 AND **TRY AGAIN**

Correct! There are millions—keep your eyes open!

You spend the night on the lookout for creepy-crawlies. It's a good thing you do, because a gigantic spider joins you in your hammock!

You check your manual—it's a tarantula!

What is the largest prey tarantulas hunt?

HUMANS!
RUN TO PAGE 30

LIZARDS AND BIRDS.
OVER TO PAGE 38

CRICKETS AND OTHER BUGS.
GO TO PAGE 18

 Poison-dart frogs are brightly colored, which signals to animals that they are poisonous.

GO BACK TO PAGE 40 AND CHOOSE AGAIN

 Bingo! Mushroom feet are not good.

Maria silently moves through the jungle. You follow her, but you keep bashing your toes on the knobbly tree roots.

Useless roots!

Roots are definitely not useless. They do something very important. Do you know what?

THEY COLLECT WATER AND NUTRIENTS.
TURN TO PAGE 22

THEY ATTRACT POLLINATING INSECTS, SUCH AS BEES.
HEAD TO PAGE 30

THEY COLLECT SUNLIGHT.
GO TO PAGE 33

TARANTULA FACTS

Tarantulas are part of the family of spiders called Hairy Mygalomorphs. The largest species of tarantula, the goliath bird-eating spider, has a leg span of up to 30 centimeters!

Yes, with showers on more than 250 days of the year, the rain forest certainly has the right name!

Suddenly, you hear a roaring sound that gets louder and louder. Around a bend in the river, you're faced with some scary-looking rapids.

To steer safely through the rapids, choose the correct route.

At what stage in its life cycle is a fish called a "fry"?

A.

B.

C.

D.

GO TO PAGE 16

TURN TO PAGE 30

OVER TO PAGE 43

GO TO PAGE 5

No, tropical hardwoods are a valuable natural resource used for buildings and furniture.

GO BACK TO PAGE 35 AND **CHOOSE AGAIN**

No, snakes and other cold-blooded animals don't have icy blood running through their veins!

GO BACK TO PAGE 23 AND **TRY AGAIN**

Correct! Mammals are the only animals to feed their young with milk.

You tell Maria that you need to continue searching for your Great Uncle. Maria suggests that you go to the village where she stays to stock up on supplies. On the way, she shows you how the shapes of some flowers fit the bodies of the animals that feed from them.

Which animal matches this plant?

HUMMINGBIRD.
TURN TO PAGE 23

BEE.
GO TO PAGE 20

BAT.
HEAD TO PAGE 9

Plants are organisms because they are alive.

GO BACK TO PAGE 23 AND **TRY AGAIN**

 Barbecued mice are tasty and nutritious.

TURN TO PAGE 42 AND **THINK AGAIN**

 That's right. As animals depend on oxygen to breathe, the rain forests are called "the lungs of the world"!

Later that evening, sitting around the fire, Dom Ignacio tells you a story.

Ramsey was not the first person to search for the Land of Gold. Some say that there is a curse on the gold—those who look for it never return.

You shiver. Before the fire goes out, you read your jungle survival guide. You'll need all the help you can get with deadly creatures AND a curse to deal with.

JUNGLE SURVIVAL GUIDE

To humans, what's the most deadly animal in the world?

ANACONDA. TURN TO PAGE 9

MOSQUITO. GO TO PAGE 17

JAGUAR. HEAD TO PAGE 20

Correct! The tallest trees reach up to the emergent layer, 200 feet high. Here they can catch the most sunlight.

Lower down, the canopy layer is home to a variety of life. Animals feed on fruit (and prey on other animals), while plants rely on animals to spread their seeds.

Look around you—the plants depend on the sun for light, and animals depend on plants for food. Bigger animals eat smaller animals. Everything is linked together in a food pyramid.

Maria quickly sketches a food pyramid.

"Two parts of this food pyramid need to be swapped around. Can you tell which ones?"

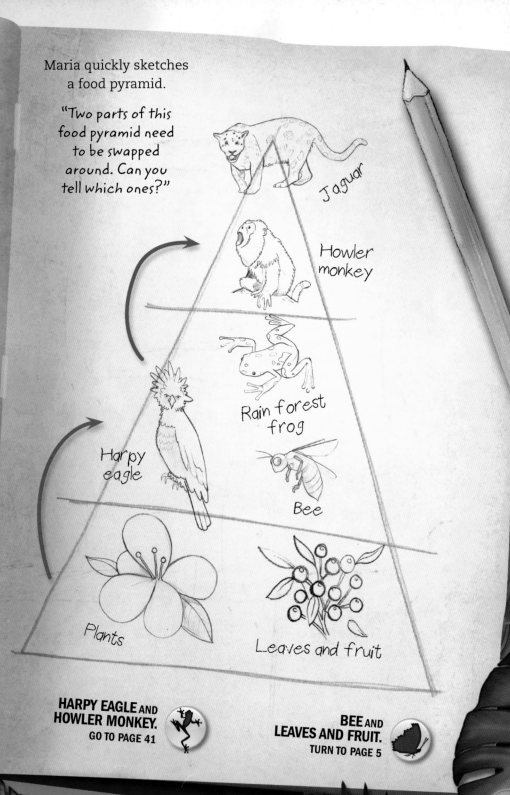

Jaguar

Howler monkey

Rain forest frog

Harpy eagle

Bee

Plants

Leaves and fruit

HARPY EAGLE AND **HOWLER MONKEY.**
GO TO PAGE 41

BEE AND **LEAVES AND FRUIT.**
TURN TO PAGE 5

Rubber is made from the sap of rubber trees that grow in the tropics.

GO BACK TO PAGE 35 AND **TRY AGAIN**

No, this is still an egg. Fish eggs take just a few days to hatch.

GO BACK TO PAGE 11 AND **TRY AGAIN**

No, germination is the process where a plant begins to grow from a seed.

TURN BACK TO PAGE 21 AND **TRY AGAIN**

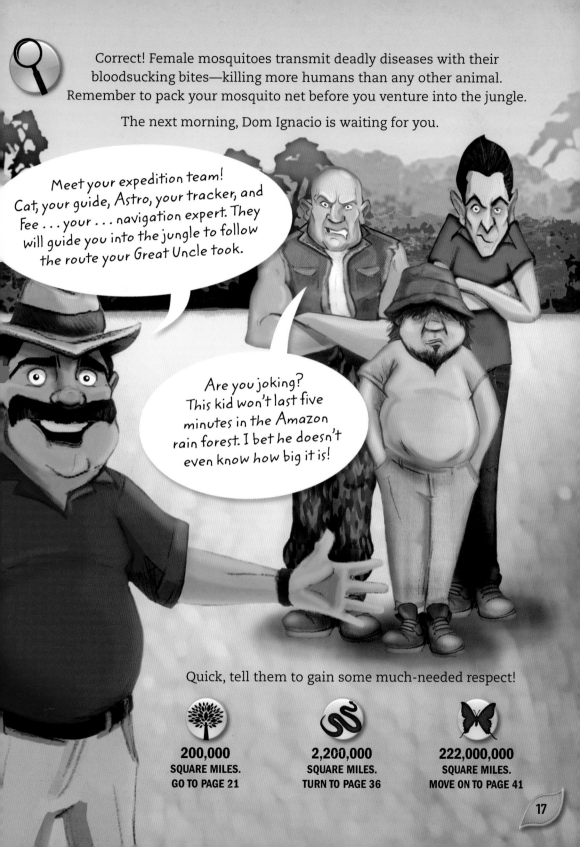

Correct! Female mosquitoes transmit deadly diseases with their bloodsucking bites—killing more humans than any other animal. Remember to pack your mosquito net before you venture into the jungle.

The next morning, Dom Ignacio is waiting for you.

Meet your expedition team! Cat, your guide, Astro, your tracker, and Fee...your...navigation expert. They will guide you into the jungle to follow the route your Great Uncle took.

Are you joking? This kid won't last five minutes in the Amazon rain forest. I bet he doesn't even know how big it is!

Quick, tell them to gain some much-needed respect!

200,000
SQUARE MILES.
GO TO PAGE 21

2,200,000
SQUARE MILES.
TURN TO PAGE 36

222,000,000
SQUARE MILES.
MOVE ON TO PAGE 41

There are a few more than six.

GO BACK TO PAGE 24
AND **LOOK AGAIN**

Of course not. Remember, rain forests are vital to the air we breathe.

GO BACK TO PAGE 42
AND **TRY AGAIN**

The goliath bird-eating spider (a type of tarantula) has fangs as big as cheetah claws. It feeds mainly on insects, but gets its name from eating hummingbirds.

GO BACK TO PAGE 10
AND **TRY AGAIN**

Bacteria are tiny living things that can only be seen through a microscope. An organism is any living thing, so that's not right.

TURN BACK
TO PAGE 23 AND **TRY AGAIN**

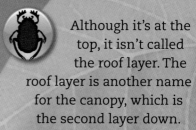 Although it's at the top, it isn't called the roof layer. The roof layer is another name for the canopy, which is the second layer down.

GO BACK TO PAGE 22 AND **TRY AGAIN**

Yes, a hungry meat eater is swimming toward you!

You move too quickly and rock the boat. The supplies tumble overboard.

Should we jump in, Astro?

Only if you want to meet the piranhas! What do you think mealtime for piranhas is called?

 SNACK ATTACK.
GO TO PAGE 23

 FEEDING FRENZY.
HEAD TO PAGE 34

 MUNCHING MAYHEM.
TURN TO PAGE 39

Many vines and plants have thorns or protective coatings that irritate the skin.

BETTER AVOID TOUCHING THEM. GO BACK TO PAGE 8 AND TRY AGAIN

The jaguar is the largest of the big cats in the jungle—but it is not the most deadly animal to humans.

GO BACK TO PAGE 13 AND TRY AGAIN

Bees prefer flowers with brightly colored landing pads, such as orchids.

GO BACK TO PAGE 12 AND TRY AGAIN

Minerals are substances found in the ground. They are essential to the life of plants and animals, but they're not alive so aren't a type of organism. Well done!

Alright brainbox, question three: In which process do plants use the sun's energy to make food and oxygen?

 PHOTOSYNTHESIS.
TURN TO PAGE 29

 OSMOSIS.
TURN TO PAGE 36

 GERMINATION.
GO TO PAGE 16

 Lemon ants are a delicacy in the Amazon, and taste just like lemon.

DIG IN AND **TURN BACK** TO PAGE 42

The Amazon is the world's largest rain forest—much larger than 200,000 square miles.

GO BACK TO PAGE 17 AND **PICK A BIGGER NUMBER**

21

? LAYER

Yes, roots collect life-giving water. They also help to keep a tree anchored in the ground.

Next, Maria takes you high into a kapok tree—a jungle giant as tall as an 18-story building!

The rain forest is divided into several layers. What is the highest layer called?

CANOPY

UNDERSTORY

FOREST FLOOR

THE ROOF LAYER.
GO TO PAGE 19

THE EMERGENT LAYER.
TURN TO PAGE 14

THE GRANDE LAYER.
HEAD TO PAGE 38

Plants must be the correct answer because Fee doesn't look happy.

Question two: Which of these is not an organism?

 **BACTERIA.**
GO TO PAGE 19

 **MINERALS.**
TURN TO PAGE 21

 **PLANTS.**
TURN TO PAGE 13

 That's right. The hummingbird's long beak easily fits down the flower's long tube.

When you reach the village, Maria gives you a package and thrusts a bunch of leaves into your hands.

 Close, but not quite.

GO BACK TO PAGE 19 AND **CHOOSE AGAIN**

Boil these and drink the water if you get bitten by a snake. It's too hot for them in the day so they mostly come out at night. That's because they're cold-blooded. Do you know what that means?

EASY! THEIR BLOOD IS AS **COLD AS ICE.**
TURN TO PAGE 12

THEY **CANNOT CONTROL** THEIR BODY TEMPERATURE.
GO TO PAGE 42

Yes, bloodsucking leeches are for cleaning wounds, not snacking on!

Eventually you come to a large waterfall. You'll have to go on foot from here. You really hope that you meet some people soon— someone who might have met your Great Uncle.

As you walk through the jungle, it feels like a thousand eyes are watching you, but you can't see anyone. Animals that live in the jungle are too well camouflaged.

How many animals can you spot?

SIX ANIMALS.
TURN TO PAGE 18

TEN ANIMALS.
GO TO PAGE 37

FIFTEEN ANIMALS.
HEAD TO PAGE 9

A man called Dom Ignacio greets you with a wide grin. He will help you on your trip.

Bem-vindo ao Brasil!
You look just like your Great Uncle. Let's see if you know as much as him. Do you know where in the world the rain forests lie?

AT THE **NORTH AND SOUTH POLES. GO TO PAGE 33**

IN A BROAD **BELT THAT CIRCLES THE TROPICS.** HEAD TO PAGE 42

IN THE **SUBTROPICAL REGIONS. TURN TO PAGE 37**

 No, birds cannot make milk. The parents of young birds bring food to the nest.

HAVE ANOTHER TRY ON PAGE 41

 Rain forest is being cut down and burned at a frightening rate—about 58,000 square miles are lost every year (the USA is 3,794,101 sq mi).

TURN BACK TO PAGE 32 AND **TRY AGAIN**

No, there are more than 100 species in your yard at home!

FLIP BACK TO PAGE 8 AND **THINK AGAIN**

 It rains more often than that! The tropical heat causes water from the rain forest to evaporate, and this moisture gathers and falls back to Earth as rain—for two thirds of the year.

TURN BACK TO PAGE 38 AND **TRY AGAIN**

 You open your eyes. Fee's hot breath is on your face and his hands are in your pockets.

What are you doing?

Um, just checking that you're okay. I'll ask you some hard questions to make sure that bump didn't do any lasting damage.

Question one: Living things are sorted into five kingdoms: animals, fungi, protists, bacteria—and what else?

PLANTS.
TURN TO PAGE 23

FISH.
GO TO PAGE 41

SPIDERS.
HEAD TO PAGE 9

Yes, push them aside with a stick. Many snakes look like vines, so you don't want to risk being bitten!

Maria takes you deep into the rain forest. Leaves block out most of the sunlight, so the forest floor is dark and cool.

Here's another question: Why is it important to keep your feet dry?

FUNGUS CAN GROW ON WET FEET. GO TO PAGE 10

YOUR FEET MAY SWELL AND NOT FIT IN YOUR BOOTS. TURN TO PAGE 39

With a shaky hand, you close your eyes, pick up the frog, and lick its back . . .

Nothing happens! You open your eyes and the Yanomami are grinning. They part to allow an old man through.

Hello! What are you doing here?

Great Uncle Ramsey!

What's going on?

TURN TO PAGE 43 **TO FIND OUT**

Correct! Plants use the sun's energy to convert carbon dioxide gas into food, releasing oxygen in the process. This is called photosynthesis.

Your mind is working fine!

Cat, Fee, and Astro start collecting firewood, but all of a sudden, they run away. A group of army ants is invading the riverbank.

Out of the blue, a woman appears from the trees, loops a rope around you, and hoists you away from the ants.

I'm Maria. My job is to study living things in the Amazon. Today I'm collecting seeds. Do you know what seeds and plants need so that they can grow?

CARBON DIOXIDE, WATER, MINERALS, AND SUNLIGHT?
GO TO PAGE 8

OXYGEN, WATER, AND SOIL?
TURN TO PAGE 37

Goliath bird-eating spiders don't feed on humans, but can give you a very nasty bite.

TURN BACK TO PAGE 10 AND **TRY AGAIN**

Delicious fruits are found all over the Amazon rain forest!

GO BACK TO PAGE 35 AND **PICK AGAIN**

Pollinating insects are attracted by bright colors and sweet smells in flowers—not by brown roots.

TURN BACK TO PAGE 10 AND **TRY AGAIN**

This is a newly hatched fish, called a larva.

GO BACK TO PAGE 11 AND **TRY AGAIN**

Rain forests have many different types of tree, with different leaf shapes.

TURN BACK TO PAGE 42 AND **TRY AGAIN**

Although plants produce oxygen, it doesn't defend them against microorganisms.

GO TO PAGE 43 AND **TRY AGAIN**

No, the caiman's not a herbivore. Teeth like that don't belong to a plant eater.

GO BACK TO PAGE 5 AND **TRY AGAIN**

Cat, Astro, and Fee appear out of the trees. They don't look happy. Fee points a spear at you as they tie your hands.

They push you along until you reach a burned, cleared area in the rain forest. In the middle is Dom Ignacio, sitting on the trunk of an enormous felled tree.

Dom Ignacio! You and your thugs have ruined my expedition to find my Great Uncle! The curse isn't real. You were just trying to stop me from discovering the damage you're doing.

Pah, I am hardly doing anything. Do you know how many square miles of rain forest are cleared every year?

AN AREA ALMOST **TWICE THE SIZE OF IRELAND.**
TURN TO PAGE 40

AN AREA **THE SIZE OF THE UNITED STATES.**
GO TO PAGE 26

Rain forests are wet, but it doesn't rain *that* much!

BACK TO PAGE 38 AND **TRY AGAIN**

 Roots are normally underground so they cannot collect sunlight. That's what a plant's leaves do.

TRY AGAIN
ON PAGE 10

 Rain forests cover a tenth of Earth's surface, but they grow best in much warmer regions. It's very cold at the poles, and few plants can grow there.

GO BACK
TO PAGE 26 AND
CHOOSE AGAIN

 No, much more than 300 swimming pools of water is carried by the Amazon every hour.

GO BACK
TO PAGE 36 AND
TRY AGAIN

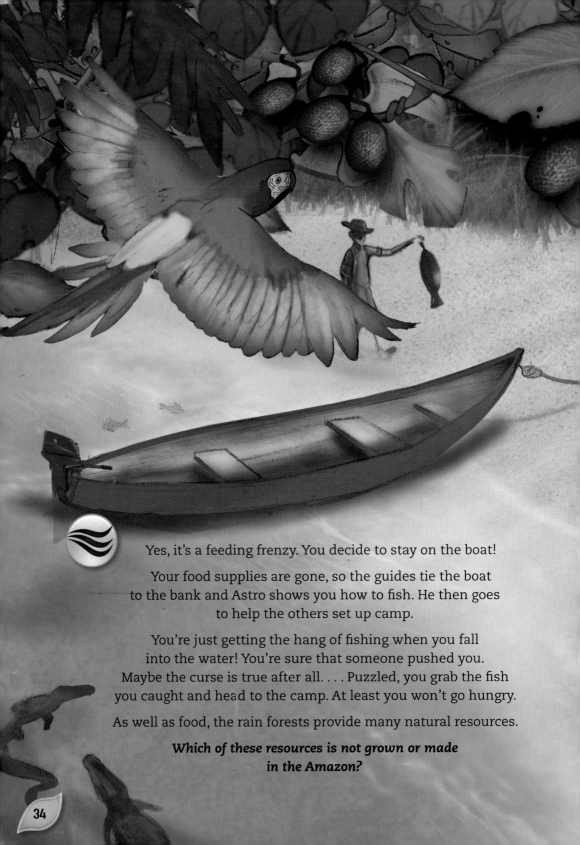

Yes, it's a feeding frenzy. You decide to stay on the boat!

Your food supplies are gone, so the guides tie the boat to the bank and Astro shows you how to fish. He then goes to help the others set up camp.

You're just getting the hang of fishing when you fall into the water! You're sure that someone pushed you. Maybe the curse is true after all. . . . Puzzled, you grab the fish you caught and head to the camp. At least you won't go hungry.

As well as food, the rain forests provide many natural resources.

Which of these resources is not grown or made in the Amazon?

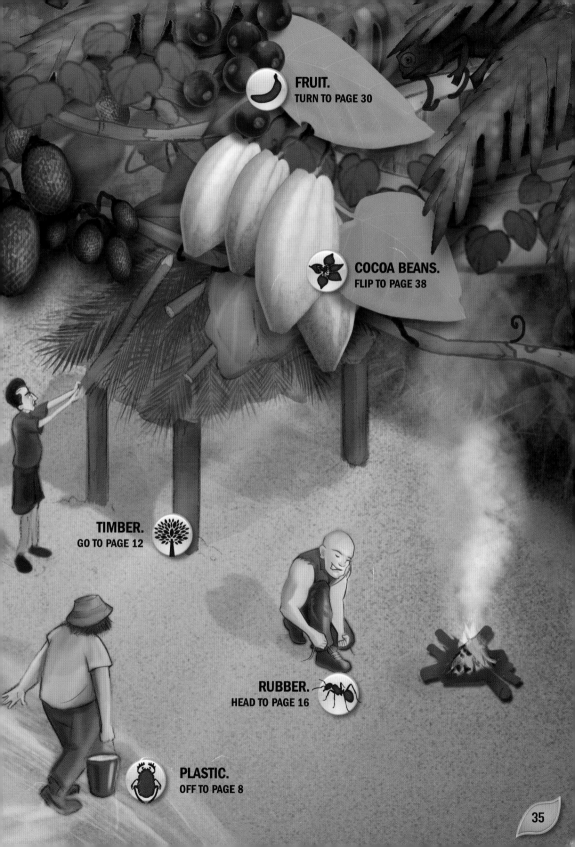

FRUIT.
TURN TO PAGE 30

COCOA BEANS.
FLIP TO PAGE 38

TIMBER.
GO TO PAGE 12

RUBBER.
HEAD TO PAGE 16

PLASTIC.
OFF TO PAGE 8

No. Plants use osmosis to draw water from their roots into their cells.

No, young insects, called larvae, mostly eat plants, fruit, and rotting things on the jungle floor.

TURN BACK TO PAGE 21 AND **HAVE ANOTHER TURN**

TURN BACK TO PAGE 21 AND **HAVE ANOTHER TURN**

GO BACK TO PAGE 41 AND **TRY AGAIN**

Exactly! It's 2.2 million square miles. Ten years ago, it was even larger, but thousands of trees are cut down every year.

The guides agree to take you. On the riverbank, Dom Ignacio smiles and waves as you travel upstream.

So, clever kid, how much water does the Amazon River carry?

EVERY HOUR, THE AMAZON TAKES **300 OLYMPIC-SIZED SWIMMING POOLS** OF WATER TO THE SEA. TURN TO PAGE 33

OF WATER TO THE SEA. TURN TO PAGE 33

EVERY HOUR, THE AMAZON TAKES **300,000 OLYMPIC-SIZED SWIMMING POOLS** OF WATER TO THE SEA. TURN TO PAGE 5

OF WATER TO THE SEA. TURN TO PAGE 5

Plants may produce oxygen, but this combination wouldn't keep a plant alive.

TRY AGAIN ON PAGE 29

A lot of rainfall is required for tall rain forest trees to grow. The subtropics are mostly dry zones.

FLIP BACK TO PAGE 26 AND **HAVE ANOTHER TRY**

Yes, there are 10 camouflaged species—and some you want to avoid!

You go deeper into the forest. There are vines in your path. You push them out of the way. Ouch! A snake bites you! You forgot to use a stick like Maria taught you.

You start to feel hot and sweaty, your legs wobble and spots dance in front of your eyes.

There's no time to lose—you must boil the leaves Maria gave you and then drink the water quickly. Saved!

There's a noise behind you. Something is running toward you very quickly . . .

WHAT NOW?! QUICK, GO TO PAGE 32

Although the tallest trees live here, it's not called the grande layer.

GO BACK TO PAGE 22 AND **TRY AGAIN**

 Cocoa beans are seeds grown in the Amazon. They're used to make chocolate.

GO BACK TO PAGE 35 AND **TRY AGAIN**

 Correct! The goliath bird-eating spider is the biggest tarantula in the world. It gets its name from hunting birds, and kills other large prey, such as lizards and rats. However, it mainly feeds on insects.

It rains all night. Wet through, you all climb back into the boat and continue upriver.

How many days a year does it rain in a tropical rain forest?

ABOUT 250 DAYS.   **ABOUT 150 DAYS.**   **ABOUT 350 DAYS.**

GO TO PAGE 11   TURN TO PAGE 27   HEAD TO PAGE 33

There are many more than 10,000 species of insect in the Amazon.

TURN BACK TO PAGE 8 AND **TRY AGAIN**

That's wrong. When cold and wet, your skin is more likely to shrink and become wrinkly!

TURN BACK TO PAGE 28

It certainly is mayhem, but this isn't the term normally used.

GO BACK TO PAGE 19 AND **TRY AGAIN**

That's right! Harpy eagles are meat-eating predators. Howler monkeys feed on fruits and insects.

Descending into the gloomy understory, you spot two tapirs—but the baby looks different from its mother.

Why is the tapir's baby striped?

To give it camouflage on the forest floor. Can you see the baby drinking its mother's milk? Only one animal group can feed its young like this —do you know which one?

The Amazon is the world's biggest rain forest—but 222 million square miles is more than the surface area of Earth!

GO BACK TO PAGE 17 AND CHOOSE ANOTHER

BIRDS. GO TO PAGE 26

MAMMALS. TURN TO PAGE 12

INSECTS. GO TO PAGE 36

Fish are part of the animal kingdom.

GO BACK TO PAGE 27 AND TRY AGAIN

Very good!
You are no fool—although there are some temperate-region rain forests too...

I bet you don't know why rain forests are sometimes called "the lungs of the world"?

FROM THE AIR, THEY ALWAYS **LOOK LIKE LUNG SHAPES.**
TURN TO PAGE 18

SUCH A VAST NUMBER OF TREES **PRODUCE HUGE QUANTITIES OF OXYGEN.**
TURN TO PAGE 13

THE LEAVES OF RAIN FOREST TREES **ARE SHAPED LIKE LUNGS.**
GO TO PAGE 31

Many poisonous snakes disguise themselves as vines. Be careful—you don't want to end up with a snakebite.

TRY AGAIN
ON PAGE 8

Correct! Cold-blooded animals warm up during the day and cool down at night. Warm-blooded animals maintain their body temperature by burning food to make heat and sweating to cool down.

You climb into a small dugout canoe and continue alone down the river. After a few hours you feel hungry, so you open the package.

Which one of these things shouldn't be eaten?

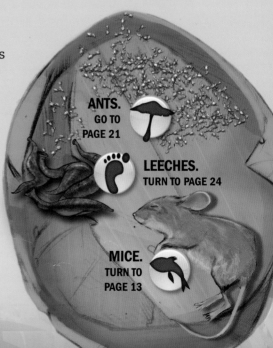

ANTS.
GO TO PAGE 21

LEECHES.
TURN TO PAGE 24

MICE.
TURN TO PAGE 13

That's right—a young fish is known as a fry.

Just as you think you're out of danger, the boat flips over. You are all tossed into the swirling waters. Your head strikes a rock. This curse is powerful!

EVERYTHING GOES BLACK. . .
TURN TO PAGE 27

 An omnivore eats plants *and* animals —the caiman isn't interested in plants!

TURN BACK TO PAGE 5 AND **CHOOSE AGAIN**

I thought you'd disappeared into the jungle!

I caught a deadly virus while looking for the Land of Gold. These people saved my life— using plants—so I stayed with them.

Do you know what plants produce to protect themselves against microorganisms?

Impress your uncle by getting this right...

OXYGEN.
GO TO PAGE 31

ANTIBACTERIAL CHEMICALS.
TURN TO PAGE 6

43

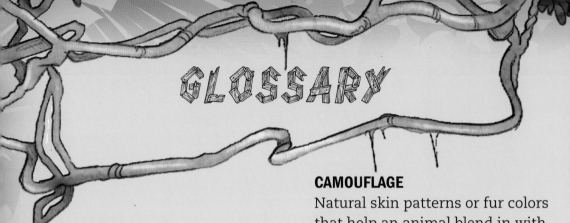

GLOSSARY

ANIMALS
One of the five kingdoms of life. An animal is a living thing that feeds on other living things— either plants or other animals. It can move and has senses such as smell and touch.

BACTERIA
One of the five kingdoms of life. A bacterium is a living thing made of a single cell.

CAMOUFLAGE
Natural skin patterns or fur colors that help an animal blend in with its surroundings. The harder an animal is to spot, the easier it is for them to avoid predators. Predators also use camouflage to sneak up on their prey, pouncing before the victim has time to escape.

CANOPY
The rain forest layer where the crowns of trees spread out, forming a nearly complete barrier of leaves and greenery, which blocks light from reaching the lower layers of the forest. Most animals live in this layer.

CARNIVORE
An animal that feeds on other animals.

COLD-BLOODED
When animals are the same temperature as their surroundings. Snakes, frogs, and fish are cold-blooded animals.

MANY RAIN FOREST SNAKES, SUCH AS BOA CONSTRICTORS, ARE CAMOUFLAGED TO MAKE THEM HARD TO SPOT.

EMERGENT LAYER

The tallest layer of a rain forest, where trees more than 200 feet tall poke above the canopy. Eagles, monkeys, bats, and butterflies live in the emergent layer.

FOOD PYRAMID

The way in which animals in a habitat are connected with each other through what they eat. Plants are always at the base of food pyramids, converting the sun's energy into food. This supplies energy for the entire food pyramid.

FOREST FLOOR

The bottom layer of a rain forest. Not much grows here because little light reaches the ground.

FUNGI

One of the five kingdoms of life, fungi feed on other organisms and reproduce by releasing spores. Mushrooms and toadstools are fungi.

HERBIVORE

An animal that only eats plants.

KINGDOM

A large group of living things that share the same basic characteristics. There are five kingdoms—bacteria, protists, fungi, plants, and animals.

MAMMAL

A warm-blooded animal that gives birth to live young and feeds them milk. Mammals live on land and in water, and include elephants, whales, bats, gorillas, and humans.

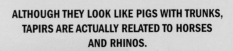

ALTHOUGH THEY LOOK LIKE PIGS WITH TRUNKS, TAPIRS ARE ACTUALLY RELATED TO HORSES AND RHINOS.

MOST LIVING THINGS ON EARTH ARE MICROORGANISMS, SMALLER THAN THE HUMAN EYE CAN SEE.

MICROORGANISM
A living thing that is too small to see without a microscope. Bacteria and amoeba (protists) are microorganisms.

NUTRIENTS
Chemicals that come from food, which are essential for the growth and development of living things.

OMNIVORE
An animal that eats both plants and animals.

ORGANISM
A living thing.

PHOTOSYNTHESIS
The process in which plants use energy from sunlight to convert carbon dioxide and water into food.

PLANTS
One of the five kingdoms of life. Green living things that make their food using photosynthesis (using energy from the sun). Trees, shrubs, grasses, ferns, and mosses are all plants.

POLLINATE
When animals transfer pollen between flowers of the same plant species. The most well known pollinator is the honeybee, but anything that visits a flower to feed can carry pollen. Rain forest pollinators include wasps, beetles, lizards, hummingbirds and other birds, as well as some small mammals.

PREY
An animal hunted and killed by another animal for food.

HUMMINGBIRDS HAVE LONG, CURVED BEAKS, WHICH ARE ESPECIALLY GOOD AT GETTING NECTAR FROM INSIDE FLOWERS.

PROTISTS

One of the five kingdoms of life, protists are mostly tiny animals with a single cell. Pond algae and tiny creatures called plankton in the sea are both types of protists.

REPTILES

Animals with scaly skin that lay eggs on dry land. Reptiles include lizards, snakes, and crocodiles.

SPECIES

A group of living things that are all very similar to each other. Species can breed with each other. Humans are members of the same species.

SUBTROPICS

The warm, dry regions of Earth next to the tropics.

TEMPERATE REGIONS

Parts of Earth where the temperatures are mild.

TROPICS

A band surrounding the middle of the planet, between the Tropic of Cancer in the north and the Tropic of Capricorn in the south. Because the sun is high in the sky all year round, the Tropics experience the hottest weather on Earth.

UNDERSTORY

Plants in the understory layer of a rain forest are short because underneath the canopy there is very little light. Many insects live here as well as large mammals such as jaguars and leopards.

WARM-BLOODED

When animals maintain their body temperature by burning food to make heat, and sweating to cool down.

TAKING IT FURTHER

The Science Quest books are designed to motivate children to develop their Science, Technology, Engineering, and Mathematics (STEM) skills. They will learn how to apply scientific know-how to the world through engaging adventure stories. For each story, readers must solve a series of scientific and technical puzzles to progress toward the exciting conclusion.

The books do not follow a page-by-page order. Instead, the reader jumps forward and backward through the book according to the answers given to the problems. If their answers are correct, the reader progresses to the next stage of the story; incorrect answers are fully explained before the reader is directed back to attempt the problem once again. Additional support is included in a full glossary of terms at the back of the book.

To support your child's scientific development you can:

- Read the book with your child.

- Continue reading with your child until he or she has understood how to follow the "Go to" instructions to the next puzzle or explanation, and is flipping through the book confidently.

- Encourage your child to read on alone. Prompt your child to tell you how the story develops and what problems he or she has solved. Take the time to ask, "What's happening now?"

- Discuss science in everyday contexts. Observe the changing seasons and how nature cycles move in step with them.

- Play STEM-based computer games with your child and choose apps that feature science topics. These hold children's interest with colorful graphics and lively animations as they discover the way the world works.

- Most of all, make science fun!